Service Writer/Advisor Basics

Charles Hillier

ISBN:
ISBN-13:9781523787081
ISBN-10:1523787082

DEDICATION

To my wife and Children who inspire me every day

CONTENTS

ACKNOWLEDGMENTS

To all my Friends that Help keep this great country
Moving

1. SKILLS REQUIRED

So, you want to be a Service Writer/Advisor. This requires three strong areas of skills:

Strong People Skills: This means having the ability to understand and effectively interact with others, as well as the ability to notice and make distinctions among the temperaments, motivations, and intentions of other people, potentially acting on this knowledge. These skills are utilized when ascertaining problems and services by listening to customers' descriptions of symptoms, clarifying problem descriptions, conducting inspections, taking test drives, checking vehicle maintenance records, and examining service schedules.

This position also requires strong **Analytical Skills** due to the need for the ability to acquire, retrieve, and store information. It also involves understanding how to transfer information and the ability to plan, make decisions, and solve problems, translating thoughts into performance. These skills are used when verifying warranty and service contract coverage by examining records and papers, explaining provisions and exclusions, preparing Repair Orders (RO) for technicians by entering RO into the service database system while describing symptoms and problems, and reviewing technician notes to determine the cause, as well as required repairs and services. It also includes developing estimates by costing materials, supplies, and labor, calculating customer payments, accounting for deductibles, and obtaining authorization and/or signatures. Additionally, maintaining accurate records by recording problems and required corrective repairs is essential.

This position also requires **Creative Skills**: the ability to solve recent problems quickly and familiar problems in an automatic way so that your mind is free to manage other issues that require insight and creativity. This skill is necessary for maintaining relationships while gaining or providing contact telephone numbers, explaining estimates and projected return dates of vehicles, arranging towing and temporary transportation if required, and answering questions and concerns while attempting to obtain customer authorizations.

2 POSITION OVERVIEW

Service Writer Job Description

Most are employed by companies offering repair services both in the private and public sectors. They also work for operators of large vehicle fleets in the transportation sector. Service writers work in vehicle service centers (shops), coordinating between customers and service technicians when vehicles need servicing or repairs and managing vehicle servicing requirements.

In smaller service centers, the service writer may also function as the service receptionist, dealing with customers at vehicle check-in and handover. Service writers ensure that a customer's needs are being fulfilled. Service writers possess product knowledge and bring efficiency to the relationship between a customer and the business. Working as a liaison for the business, an effective service writer brings competence to a customer's experience by coordinating the transaction.

Qualifications

Although product knowledge and experience are preferred by most employers, service writers do not require formal education requirements beyond a minimum of a high school diploma.

They must have detailed knowledge of the workings of a vehicle, so they understand customers' problems or instructions. Knowledge of office computer programs, such as Microsoft Office, is often a requirement. as there are portions of the customer profile that need to be entered into a computer system.

Service writers can improve their product knowledge by

taking a course in vehicle technology offered by manufacturers or colleges.

There are technical programs that offer a curriculum that is centered on the technical aspects of vehicle repair, such as braking, electrical, and suspension systems. Some colleges offer an associate degree that can enhance a potential service writer's product knowledge and expertise. Earning a degree is not a requirement, but can be a way to gain product knowledge before employment

Customer Liaison

Service writers meet customers who need scheduled servicing or repairs, discuss the customers' requirements, and translate those requirements into instructions for service technicians. They provide the customer with an estimate of costs and indicate when the vehicle will be ready for collection. If the vehicle requires additional work beyond the original estimate, the service writer contacts the customer to advise the extra cost and obtain approval to proceed.

Job duties for a service writer revolve around the needs of the customer. They develop relationships with customers through successful management of product or service delivery. Their duties can include tracking repairs and their causes, scheduling technicians, and processing warranties. Customer profile information is usually stored in a computer system, which the service writer is responsible for maintaining.

Administration

Service writers enter the details of the job on the service center computer system and prepare detailed instructions for the service technicians together with a list of the replacement parts needed for the job. If the job has a standard time allowance, they advise the service technician. They also check the vehicle's warranty or extended warranty to see if any repairs are covered by insurance. Additional duties of a service writer involve developing cost estimates. When a customer requests a repair, the service writer logs what parts are needed, and how much time should be allocated to repair and schedules the appropriate technician for the job based on the customer and their repair needs. This information is conveyed to both the customer and the employer of the service writer in a timely fashion.

Customer Satisfaction

When the job is complete, service writers hand the vehicle back to the customer, explaining the work that has been conducted. The service writer's customer liaison role plays an important part in building customer satisfaction, which is critical to building repeat business for the service center. The service writer's ability to interpret vehicle problems correctly, ensure that technicians complete the work effectively, and explain work and costs to customers clearly and openly are crucial factors in customers' perceptions of a service center.

Service Revenue

Service writers also can make an important contribution to service revenue growth. They monitor customers' records to check when scheduled servicing is due and contact them to arrange appointments. By arranging a thorough inspection of the vehicle when it is in the service center, service writers may be able to identify remedial work that needs to be conducted in the future. They advise the customer when they hand back the vehicle or contact the customer earlier if the remedial work is urgent. This helps to generate additional revenue and demonstrates elevated levels of customer care.

THE FOCUS

Now that you have accepted the job and understand the requirements, as a service writer, there are a few things that you will need to focus on.

Number one is the needs of your customers; this is the most important item you need to focus on. The whole repair industry is driven by the needs of the customer - without them, you would be unemployed. Keep in mind that no one is excited about having to bring their vehicle in for service. Even when scheduled, most people have other things they would rather be doing. They all need to have their vehicles repaired on time at a reasonable price.

The challenge is that a timely manner and a reasonable cost may mean different things to different people. You, having some basic knowledge of repairs, have one perspective, while the customer may have another. This is where your communication skills are vital.

Keep in mind that only you know your facility's workload, the amount of time the repairs should take, and the parts involved. So, the customer is informed about the time required and the cost involved. Once you tell the customer, you must keep your agreement. If, for some reason, you cannot, you need to communicate this to the customer immediately. Failure to satisfy the needs of the customer will result in poor customer satisfaction.

Sadly, this is where most of the time the process goes wrong. Whether the parts are delayed, the technician calls in, or the repair goes sideways, these issues can be communicated to the customer, and a resolution can be agreed upon. But sadly, we all have come to pick up the vehicle only to be told that it is either not ready, the bill is higher than agreed to, or the concern is still unresolved. Regardless of all your excellent work to develop a good relationship, it has now been undermined.

The next thing you need to focus on is the wants of your customers. Most people agree that there are some universal wants. When customers were asked, "What do you want from your service department?" the number one response was to get in and out as soon as possible. This can be as simple as always having someone in the service drive to help the customer with dropping off their vehicle, but this does not always happen. The following is a true account posted online by an irate customer.

It all started when "Joe's" yellow engine lamp came on. He figured that he would stop and get it checked out at his local repair shop. They advertised a free check of the check engine lamp, so he thought he would give them a chance. It was 11:00 am by the time he arrived. The shop had a few people picking up their vehicles, so he waited his turn.

While waiting, he overheard the service writers talking about getting lunch but thought nothing of it until he noticed that one by one, the writers disappeared. When the last pickup was done, the service writer who was taking care of them just walked into the back room and paid no attention to him. When he asked the mechanics where everyone had gone, they told him it was lunchtime, and he would need to wait. Joe went back into his car and left. If the writers had just taken his information down, they may have gained a customer. The only thing the repair shop received was a scathing online rebuke for everyone to see.

The next universal need is to have alternative transportation available so customers can get on with their lives. This is important if they need to leave the vehicle for more than a few hours. Whether it is as simple as a ride to work and then being picked up, a loaner vehicle, or even having a rental company that is willing to rent to your customers, the availability of a way to continue with their day is important in today's environment.

4 CUSTOMERS CHECK-IN

As a service advisor, it is important to follow a systematic process when checking in customers and their vehicles. Here is a step-by-step breakdown of the process:

1. Greet the customer: Welcome the customer to the facility and introduce yourself by stating your name. For example, "Welcome to (facilities name), my name is (your name), and I will be checking your vehicle in." Ensure the customer acknowledges your introduction.

2. Determine the reason for the visit: Ask the customer what brings them to the facility. Their response will help you understand the nature of the repair needed and categorize it into one of three types:

- Maintenance repairs: These are routine maintenance tasks or promotional items that can typically be completed within the same day. The customer may choose to wait or drop off the vehicle and return before closing.

- Minor repairs: These repairs may take a few hours or overnight. They may require parts that are not currently in stock but can be obtained by the next day. It is important to diagnose the issue before the end of the day and provide the customer with a call back for the diagnosis and repair estimate. In some cases, a short-term loaner vehicle or arrangements for a ride home may be necessary.

- Major repairs: These are typically more extensive repairs, often involving a vehicle that has been towed in. Major repairs may require longer-term rental or loaner vehicles and parts that may take several days to acquire.

3. Perform initial vehicle inspection: As you begin checking the vehicle in, carefully note or photograph any

existing body damage or obvious issues. This documentation is important for protecting you and your employer from potential liability or lawsuits. If any issues are identified, address them with the customer and ensure they are aware of the existing condition.

4. Identify safety issues: Inform the customer of any noticeable safety concerns on their vehicle. This includes checking all the lamps, such as turn signals, flashers, and brake lights. If possible, inspect the windshield wipers as well.

5. Conduct an interview: Allow the customer to express their concerns about the vehicle. Ask specific questions regarding when the issue occurs, the speeds or conditions under which it can be duplicated, and any other relevant details. This information will assist in the diagnosis and repair process.

6. Confirm customer concerns: Once the interview is completed, summarize the customer's concerns and read them back to ensure accuracy. This helps validate that the concerns are correctly understood and that no additional work is being requested. Request the customer's signature on the repair order, which signifies their authorization for you to work on the vehicle, and accept responsibility for any charges incurred during the repair.

Note: The customer's signature is crucial, as it serves as a formal release and agreement for you to drive and work on the vehicle. It also acknowledges the customer's commitment to pay for the services rendered. In case of non-payment, it provides you with the ability to place a lien on the vehicle or seek the title for selling it to recover costs.

7. Address the customer's main concern: Prioritize addressing the customer's main concern above anything else. Ensure that the concern is diagnosed, documented, and addressed with the customer before proceeding to any other issues. Avoid trying to sell additional services until the primary concern has been addressed.

8. Document the repair order: It is essential to accurately document the cause of the failure, the repair actions taken, and the agreed-upon amount for the repair. The technician's notes should be clear and concise, avoiding excessive use of industry jargon. Remember that the customer may not be familiar with technical terms, so explanations should be easy to understand.

By following these steps, you can ensure a systematic and customer-focused approach to checking in vehicles and initiating the repair process.

5 THE REPAIR ORDER

The repair order is a crucial document that serves as a legal and binding representation of the repairs performed and the communication between you and the customer. Here are some important points regarding the repair order:

1. Complete and accurate information: Ensure that all required fields on the repair orders are filled out completely and accurately. This includes identifying the vehicle, noting the time and date of services rendered, and documenting any authorizations or refusals of repairs by the customer.

2. Documenting interactions: It is vital to document any interactions between you and the customer, including the time, date, and content of conversations. Whether authorizations were given through text, email, or phone calls, make sure to have records that reflect these conversations. Print off and attach any approvals given via text messages or emails to the repair order.

3. Transferring information: Start the repair process by transferring all necessary information from the write-up form to the actual repair order system. This includes entering the vehicle information, customer concerns, mileage, time, dates, and a clear and complete description of the owner's concerns and instructions to the technician. Assign a separate line for each customer concern and use basic abbreviations when necessary.

4. Review by a technician: Once the repair order is logged into the management system, it is assigned to the technician. The technician should review the repair order, paying special attention to the customer's concerns. They should ask themselves if there is enough information to

begin an accurate diagnosis of the vehicle. If not, they should consult with the advisor to gather additional information.

5. Reasonable and necessary services: The repair order should only include repairs that are considered "reasonable and necessary" for diagnosing and repairing the malfunctioning system/part. These services must be safe, effective, consistent with the symptoms and diagnosis, and adhere to accepted professional standards and repair procedures.

6. Unreasonable and unnecessary services: Conversely, the repair order should not include services that are deemed "unreasonable and unnecessary." These may be services that are not accepted as safe and effective, lack authoritative evidence, are experimental, not necessary, excessive in duration or frequency, not performed according to accepted standards, or performed in an inappropriate setting.

7. Additional repairs and authorizations: If additional repairs are required beyond the initial write-up or not covered in the original order, prepare an estimate for the added cost and contact the customer for permission to proceed. Document the additional authorization, including the method of communication (verbal, telephone, fax, or email), and attach any necessary supporting documents, such as a signed and dated fax or a copy of the email authorization.

By ensuring that the repair order is accurately completed, documenting all interactions and authorizations, and adhering to the principles of reasonable and necessary services, you can maintain a transparent and legally sound record of the repairs performed.

6 ANGRY CUSTOMERS

Dealing with angry customers can be challenging, but it's essential to handle the situation effectively to maintain a good relationship and potentially turn them into repeat customers. Here are some tips for managing angry customers:

1. Listen and show empathy: Allow the customer to express their frustration and actively listen to their concerns. Show understanding by saying things like, "I understand completely, and I'm sorry you're upset. Let's find a way to work this out." Using inclusive language like "let's" portrays you and the customer as a team working together to find a solution.

2. Respond with empathy: Reiterate the customer's complaint and respond with empathy. Use phrases like, "That sounds incredibly frustrating" or "I'd feel the same way in your shoes." It's important to empathize without necessarily giving in to all of their demands. Remember, it's you and the customer against the problem, not the customer against you and your company.

3. Remain calm and professional: Set aside your ego and remember that other people may be observing the interaction. Stay calm, speak clearly, and lower your voice. Emotions are contagious, so maintaining a composed demeanor will help defuse the situation.

4. Understand the root of the anger: Try to understand the underlying cause of the customer's anger by sorting through their emotions. Stay positive, acknowledge their feelings, show a willingness to help, and work together to find a resolution.

5. Apologies without patronizing: Offer a sincere apology on behalf of the company, expressing regret that the customer was not satisfied. Avoid apologizing in a way that belittles or diminishes the customer's emotions. Apologize for your actions or those of the company, not for the way the customer feels.

6. Involve your manager if necessary: If the situation is escalating or you're unable to resolve the issue, notify your manager. They have more authority to address the customer's concerns, potentially offering discounts or concessions. Involving a higher authority can also provide reassurance to the customer that their issue will be taken seriously.

7. Provide a comfortable waiting area: If you need to fetch your manager or handle the situation further, offer the customer a comfortable place to wait away from other customers if possible. If authorized, offer refreshments such as water. Small gestures of kindness can help calm down an upset customer.

8. Be honest about what you can deliver: Only promise what you can realistically deliver. Offering solutions or promises you can't fulfill will only further frustrate the customer. If unsure, consult your supervisor before making any decisions under pressure.

9. Don't take it personally: Remember not to take the complaints personally. Stay focused on addressing the problem and aim to end the interaction on a positive note. Express gratitude for the customer's patience and assure them that steps will be taken to ensure a smoother experience in the future.

10. Handle intoxicated customers: If a customer is intoxicated or under the influence of drugs and becomes disruptive or poses a safety risk, prioritize the safety and well-being of yourself and others. Call for security or take appropriate measures to handle the situation without wasting time trying to reason with them.

Remember, difficult customers are potential opportunities for improvement and growth. By effectively addressing their concerns, you have the chance to turn their negative experience into a positive one. A satisfied customer is more likely to share their positive experience, which can lead to more potential customers.

7 FIRST IMPRESSION

Personal appearance and first impressions have a significant impact on customer interaction. Here are some key points highlighting the importance of personal appearance and first impressions:

People often form quick judgments based on initial impressions, including appearance. How an individual presents themselves physically can influence how they are perceived by others. Dressing appropriately, grooming well, and maintaining a professional appearance can help create a positive perception.

In any professional setting, personal appearance plays a crucial role in establishing credibility and professionalism. A well-groomed and appropriately dressed individual is more likely to be seen as competent, trustworthy, and reliable. It can also impact career opportunities, promotions, and professional relationships.

Having a positive first impression contributes to building trust and confidence. When meeting someone for the first time, a professional appearance can instill a sense of trust and make others feel more comfortable. This is particularly important in customer-facing roles, where customers are more likely to have confidence in individuals who present themselves well.

Personal appearance can significantly impact customer satisfaction and loyalty. Customers often associate a well-groomed and professional appearance with a high level of service quality. On the other hand, a disheveled or unprofessional appearance can create doubts about the competence and reliability of the service provider.

A personal appearance is a form of non-verbal communication that conveys messages about an individual's personality, attention to detail, and self-respect. This may influence how others perceive an individual's level of professionalism, confidence, and approachability.

Your appearance also reflects the image and values of your organization. You are the face of the company, and your appearance contributes to the overall brand representation.

First impressions are often lasting impressions. People tend to remember their initial encounters and form opinions that can be challenging to change later. A negative first impression due to a poor personal appearance may result in missed opportunities or difficulties in building positive relationships.

It is important to note that while personal appearance and first impressions are significant, they should not overshadow the importance of skills, knowledge, and behavior. A combination of a professional appearance, competence, and a positive attitude is the ideal approach to making a lasting positive impact on others.

Maintaining a clean and organized work area is also essential. Cluttered or messy surroundings can create a negative impression. Take the time to keep your workspace tidy and free of excessive promotional materials.

As the face of the facility and the first point of contact, it's crucial to adhere to any dress code policies set by the repair facility. Remember that your appearance and behavior reflect the professionalism of the organization. First impressions matter, and you want to make a positive impact on customers.

Mind your manners when interacting with customers. Address them as "sir" or "ma'am" until you have their name, and then use Mr. or Ms. followed by their last name. Avoid addressing them by their first name unless specifically instructed to do so. Show utmost respect to customers, as they are not your friends but individuals who deserve your professional courtesy.

Give customers your undivided attention when they are speaking to you. Their time is valuable, and unless it's an emergency, everything else can wait. Focus on actively listening and providing assistance to their needs.

Lastly, treat customers' vehicles with care and respect. Just as you would treat the owners of your shop's vehicles, ensure that customer vehicles are handled with attention to detail and consideration. If possible, offer a wash after service, as customers appreciate a clean vehicle. This practice is often followed by new car dealerships during servicing.

Always remember that the customer is the priority. It's your responsibility to make a great first impression, as it can significantly impact the customer's perception of the repair facility and their willingness to return for future service.

ABOUT THE AUTHOR

The author of this text is an individual with extensive experience in the automotive industry. They have completed their education at Elgin Community College and have worked in various roles within retail repair facilities, including serving as a shop supervisor and service manager in Batavia, IL, and Wheaton, IL. They are a certified instructor for the state of Illinois and have worked with organizations such as AYES (Automotive Youth Educational Systems) and NATEF (National Automotive Technicians Education Foundation) in certifying high schools.

The author is a Master Certified ASE (Automotive Service Excellence) Technician, holding certifications in automotive, truck, and bus repairs. They are currently employed by a global manufacturing company where their responsibilities include managing North America dealer labor rates, regional warranty training, and administration.

In addition to their practical experience, the author has written and published several works related to the automotive industry and has also presented and spoken at industry conferences. Their expertise and knowledge in the field make them a credible source on topics related to automotive repairs, service management, and customer relations.